What makes People different?

Susan Meredith

Designed by Lindy Dark
Illustrated by Annabel Spenceley and Kuo Kang Chen
Consultants: Dr Michael Hitchcock, Indu Patel and Dr John Kesby
Cover design by Russell Punter
Cover illustration by Christyan Fox
With thanks to Sarah Cronin

CONTENTS

What is a person?

Have you ever wondered why you are what you are? Why are you the same as other people in so many ways, yet different as well?

People everywhere are like they are for two main reasons. One is that they take after their parents. The other is that they are affected by the sort of life they lead.

There are millions of different kinds of living things in the world.

What made you a person, not some other living thing like a cat or a daisy, are thousands of tiny things inside you called genes. People's genes are different from animal or plant genes.

Where you live

Your genes are only part of the story. You are also the way you are because of where you live: your surroundings. Another word for surroundings is environment. Your environment affects the way you live.

This picture shows life in a part of West Africa.

These women are pounding vegetables called yams. They are made into a kind of porridge.

Young children stay close to their mothers.

This woman is carrying pots.

*Pictures with the symbol ☐ can be downloaded from **www.usborne-quicklinks.com***

You got, or inherited, your genes from your parents.

Your parents inherited their genes from their parents.

Genes are the instructions which make your body work in the way it does. Everyone gets their genes from their parents, at the moment when they start to grow inside their mother.

Some things about you, like the way you look, depend a lot on your genes.

People all look different because of their genes.

Although everybody has genes, they are arranged in a different pattern in different people. That is one of the reasons why one person is not quite like another.

One big family

Everyone everywhere is really part of the same huge family which scientists call humans or human beings.

Everyone's bodies and brains are made in the same way.

Overhanging thatch keeps rain off the walls.

Houses are made of mud bricks which have been dried in the sun. They are cool inside.

The weather is hot. Long, loose cotton clothes help people keep cool.

Oven

Internet link Go to **www.usborne-quicklinks.com** for a link to a website where you can watch movies about genes and heredity.

3

Where did people come from?

Jellyfish have been around for hundreds of millions of years; people for only about two million.

Creatures which were a bit like small apes lived about 10 million years ago.

There have not always been people in the world. There were plants and animals long before any humans. So where did people come from?

Most scientists think that living things gradually change, or evolve, over a very long time. They think people evolved from ape-like creatures.*

Out of Africa

Experts think that the first people evolved in Africa. They think they gradually spread all over the world from there, in the directions of the arrows on this map.

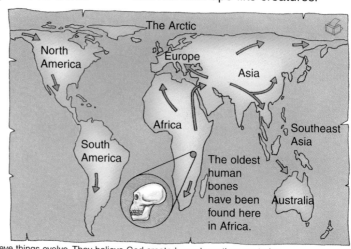

The Arctic

North America

Europe

Asia

Africa

Southeast Asia

South America

The oldest human bones have been found here in Africa.

Australia

*Some people do not believe things evolve. They believe God created people as they are today.

4

The first people

The humans who lived two million years ago walked on two legs and had hands which could use tools. They hunted animals and gathered wild plant foods.

Our oldest relations

The first people whose bodies and brains were like ours evolved about a hundred thousand years ago.

Young humans are very much like young chimps.

Chimps

The animals people are most like today are chimps. Nine out of every ten human genes are almost the same as chimp genes. The main difference is that people are brainier.

They made many weapons and tools, and could probably talk. This picture shows life in a cool place.

These people hunted with spears.

They lived in caves and in shelters made from animal skins.

They made fires: for warmth, for cooking and to frighten off wild animals.

They sewed animal skins to wear.

Internet link Go to **www.usborne-quicklinks.com** for a link to a website where you can see the stages in human evolution.

5

Taking after your parents

The genes you get from your parents control the way your body lives, works and grows. The picture below shows just a few of the things about you that depend on your genes.

Your hair: whether it is dark or fair, curly or straight.

Your voice

Your eye colour

Your face

Your skin colour

The way you live cannot change your genes. It can affect how your body copes with some genes though.

Some people seem to inherit genes which make them more at risk of tooth decay than others.

If they do not eat much sweet food and clean their teeth very thoroughly, their teeth may stay healthy.

How genes work

Most things about you are decided by several genes. A few, such as hair and eye colour, depend mainly on one gene from each parent. The example on the right will give you an idea of how genes work.

Your hair colour depends on the mixture of your two hair colour genes. A dark hair gene is dominant (strong). It blocks out genes for other colours. A fair hair gene blocks out a red hair gene.

Jessica's mother has a dark and a red hair gene. Her dark gene blocks out her red gene.

Jessica's father has a fair and a red hair gene. His fair gene blocks out the red one.

Jessica happened to inherit both her mother's and father's red hair genes.

What are your genes?

Your body is made of millions of tiny living parts called cells. Your genes are stored in your cells, on special threads called chromosomes.

There are 46 chromosomes in each of your cells: 23 from your mother, 23 from your father.

Cell

Chromosome

Chromosomes are made of a chemical (DNA) which looks like a twisted ladder. There are hundreds of genes on each chromosome.

About 250 rungs on the ladder make one gene.

The rungs are arranged in a different order in different people. This is what makes everybody unique.

Exactly which of your parents' genes you get seems to be a matter of chance. That is why brothers and sisters do not always seem alike.

Only identical twins have exactly the same genes.

Genes or environment?

Simon walks with his feet turned out. Is this because of his genes or because he has copied his Dad? Nobody knows.

There is a lot that is still not known about genes. Nobody really knows whether some things about you depend mainly on your genes, your environment or both.

Internet link Go to *www.usborne-quicklinks.com* for a link to a website with fun activities to find out more about genes.

People and the weather

Living things evolve (change) to fit in with their environment. This is called adapting to the environment. Things that do not adapt, die.

Things that do adapt, survive and pass on their genes to their children. Gradually there come to be more and more of the well adapted things.

Woolly mammoths were well suited to life in the ice age. When the weather warmed up, they did not adapt and died out.

Humans evolved skilful hands and good brains. This makes them well adapted to their environment.

Body build

Over a very long time, people's genes have helped them adapt to the weather in different parts of the world.

All people have a layer of fat under their skin, which helps protect them from the cold.

In cold places, people often have a thicker layer of fat, which helps keep them warm.

In families that have lived in cold places for a long time, people have adapted. The people who had more fat were more likely to survive the cold. They passed on their genes to their children.

These people live in the Arctic, where it is very cold.

Internet link Go to *www.usborne-quicklinks.com* for a link to a website with quiz games about people and weather in different parts of the world.

Dark or fair skin?

In very sunny places people evolved dark skin. This blocks out some of the Sun's harmful rays.

Dark skin helps to protect people from too much sun.

In cloudier places people did not need so much protection from the sun. They evolved fairer skin.

People need some sunshine because it gives them vitamin D.

Ways of life

It is not only people's genes which have adapted to the weather. People have also adapted their way of life. Clothes, houses, even food and jobs can all depend on the weather.

A headdress and veil give protection from the sun and wind of the Sahara Desert.

Houses are built on stilts in Southeast Asia, where there are often floods.

Living apart

Groups of people came to look different not only because of the weather but also because they lived far apart.

In the past, people did not tend to travel far, so they did not meet people from other parts of the world.

Today people from opposite sides of the world marry each other. Their genes get mixed together in their children.

9

Learning to fit in

Right from the time you are a baby, you have to start learning to fit in with the people around you. Different people have to learn to fit into very different kinds of worlds, depending on where they are growing up.

Showing the soles of your feet when you are sitting down is very impolite in Arab countries.

Eating in public places is impolite in Japan.

How you are expected to behave depends on your own family's way of thinking and on the general ways and rules of the place where you live.

Masai women, in East Africa, shave their heads.

Young Masai men have long hair.

Men and women wear necklaces and earrings.

Someone who likes being outdoors may not much enjoy city life.

How you dress depends on what people in the place where you live think is suitable and attractive.

How happily people fit in depends on the kind of person they are and the type of environment they live in.

How do people learn?

Children learn to behave by following the example of people they admire such as parents, teachers and friends.

Behaving well is sometimes rewarded by smiles, praise or even presents. This encourages someone to be good another time.

Babies

Young babies do not fit in all that well with other people. When they need something, they just cry for it. This is the only way they have to tell people something is wrong.

Babies cannot wait for things, or imagine how other people feel.

Children

As babies grow up, they learn to fit in, for example, eating at mealtimes, not just when they are hungry.

At school, you learn skills which will help you to cope with life in the wider world outside your family.

You also learn by playing with other children, for example, how to share and take turns in games.

Making a living

Internet links Go to **www.usborne-quicklinks.com** for links to websites where you can find out how a goat can help a Kenyan village and meet farmers around the world.

People everywhere need things like food and shelter. Most people have to earn money to meet their needs. The work people do depends largely on where they live and what kind of jobs there are in the area.

Farming

Around half of the people in the world live in villages rather than towns.

In some parts of the world machines are used.

Harvesting in America.

Harvesting rice in Southeast Asia.

In places where most people are farmers (Africa, Asia, South America) a lot of work is still done by hand.

Farmers often have large families so there are plenty of people to help with the work, including the children.

Factory work

In places like Europe, North America, Japan and Australia there is a lot of industry. Many people work in factories, making things to be sold, or in offices. They get paid a wage.

People in industrial places often live in small families. They may move to find work.

In some places farmers do not get paid but keep some of what they grow.

12

Herding animals

In a few places, where it is too dry to do much else, some people herd animals for a living. They have to keep moving from place to place to find water and grazing land for the animals. These people are called nomads. They get most of what they need from their animals.

These people in Central Asia live in felt tents. (Felt is made from animals' wool.)

The tents are warm, and can be taken down and moved fairly easily.

The people keep sheep, goats, yaks, horses and camels. They sell animals to buy things they need such as wheat.

From the animals they get meat, milk and cheese; and wool and skins to make into clothes, tents and blankets.

They use the animals for getting around.

Fishing

Some people by the sea depend on fishing for their living, especially in places where there is no farming or industry nearby.

In the Arctic it is too cold for crops to grow. This man is fishing through a hole in the ice.

Other jobs

Some jobs are done all over the world, for example, teaching, nursing, or office work. Others are only done in certain places.

Tea will only grow on hills in warm wet places. It is grown in India and China.

Picking tea

13

Talking to each other

There are thousands of different languages spoken in the world today. The languages with the most speakers are English and Chinese.

How did language begin?

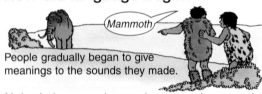

People gradually began to give meanings to the sounds they made.

Nobody is sure when or how people started to talk. They may have begun with noises such as grunts, and signs such as pointing.

Borrowing words

As people move around the world, their language goes with them. Words from one language often creep into another. Below are just a few words which have come into English from other languages.

potato (Native American), *anorak* (Inuit), *tea* (Chinese), *jungle* (Hindi), *garage* (French), *pyjamas* (Urdu), *orange* (Arabic), *robot* (Czech), *coach* (Hungarian).

Body language

In Indonesia it is rude to point with your finger. People use their thumb.

You do not only talk in words. You also use your face and body. Some things, like laughing and crying, mean the same everywhere. Some do not.

Language families

Guten Morgen — German
Good morning — English
Goede morgen — Dutch

Many languages are related. French, Spanish and Italian all evolved from Latin, the language of the Ancient Romans. English is similar to German and Dutch.

Learning to talk

By the time they are one, most babies can speak a few words and understand many more.

Babies' babblings include all the sounds it is possible for the human voice to make.

Young children gradually learn to speak the same language as their parents just by hearing and copying the sounds they make.

Same but different

The same language is often spoken differently in different places.

Even the same person can speak differently in different situations. Do you talk the same way to your friends as you do to your teachers?

Writing

There are over 50 different alphabets. Most West European languages have used the Roman alphabet since the time the Romans were rulers. On the right are some letters from different alphabets.

Chinese does not have an alphabet like that of most other languages.

This one symbol means horse in Chinese.

15

Moving around

Right from the time the first people moved out of Africa, groups of people have left one area and gone to settle in another. Journeys made long ago help to explain why people live where they do now.

Hunger

Sometimes people move because their crops die through drought (lack of rain), floods or disease.

In 1845, the potato crop in Ireland failed and people were starving. Thousands left for America or England.

Where from?

As people move around, they take their ideas and the things they use with them. Here are a few examples of where things started out.

Guinea pigs Potatoes }	South America
Fireworks Ice Cream }	China
Arithmetic Oranges }	The Middle East

Slavery

In the 1600s and 1700s, millions of Africans were forced to go to America and work as slaves in the fields where sugar, tobacco and cotton were grown.

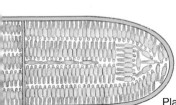

Huge numbers of slaves were packed into ships for the journey to America. Many of them died.

Plan of a slave ship.

Jobs

People often move from the countryside into towns to find work. Sometimes they move to a completely foreign country, often one which has close links with their own.

In the 1950s, many doctors moved from India to Britain, where more doctors were needed.

Power

There have been many times when one group of people has moved in on another and tried to rule them.

In the 1500s, Spain conquered many parts of South and Central America and ruled them for years.

Spanish is still spoken in those countries (shown yellow on this map), making it the third most spoken language in the world.

Brazil (Portuguese spoken here.)

Land

Sometimes people have moved to find new land to live on and farm. This has often led to trouble.

In the 1800s, many Europeans went to North America. There were fierce battles as they tried to take land there.

European settlers

Native Americans

The Native Americans were pushed into living only in certain areas called reservations.

Disagreements

Sometimes people are badly treated just because of what they believe or even who they are. This often happens in wartime.

Many Jews fled from Central and Eastern Europe at the time of World War II to escape being killed.

Prisoners

In 1788, the British government began sending prisoners far from home to Australia as a punishment.

Many stayed and made their living in Australia when their time in prison was over.

What people believe

People's beliefs depend a lot on what their families believe and on the religion and ideas that are taught in the place where they grow up. There are many different religions. Some have a lot in common.

Festivals

The Japanese Shinto religion teaches that gods are in nature.

People pray at places like this.

Many religions involve believing in some kind of god or gods. Believers may pray to their god, often asking for help or giving praise and thanks.

Religions try to explain how the world and people were made. It is only fairly recently that scientists have worked out the idea that living things evolved.*

The Christian and Jewish religions teach that God made the world and the first man and woman: Adam and Eve.

This Muslim is going from door to door, collecting rice for the poor.

Religions give rules for how to behave. For example, Muslims are expected to give to the poor and old.

18 *See page 4.

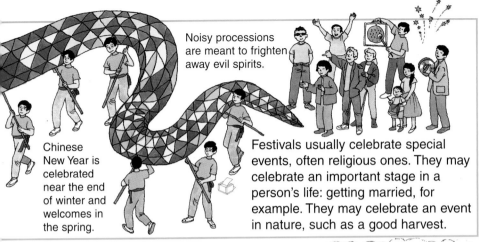

Noisy processions are meant to frighten away evil spirits.

Chinese New Year is celebrated near the end of winter and welcomes in the spring.

Festivals usually celebrate special events, often religious ones. They may celebrate an important stage in a person's life: getting married, for example. They may celebrate an event in nature, such as a good harvest.

Many religions involve believing in some kind of life after death. Hinduism, for example, teaches that people are reborn into the world. If you are good in this life, your next life will be a better one.

Hindu holy men give up their possessions and try to live a good and simple life.

Politics

People with different political ideas disagree about the best way to organize and rule a country.

Environmentalists believe it is all-important to improve the environment before it is totally ruined.

In some places people have no say in who rules them. In most countries elections are held. Then people can vote for those they think will run the country best.

Voting in India

Internet links Go to www.usborne-quicklinks.com for links to websites where you can find out about religious festivals and holidays around the world.

19

People in groups

People everywhere are much more alike than they are different. However, it is sometimes interesting to think about people as different groups.

Male and female

Without the bodily differences between men and women, human beings would soon die out because no babies would be made.

What makes the difference between a boy and a girl is just one chromosome out of the 46 you have in each cell in your body.

The way men and women behave differently and do different tasks has a lot to do with where they live and how they were brought up.

In Bali, Southeast Asia, women do the heavy work on building sites.

Ethnic groups

People of the same ethnic group have relations who lived in the same part of the world long ago. They often share the same language, customs and beliefs.

In Australia, a lot of people whose relations originally came from Britain eat British Christmas dinner.

Internet link Go to www.usborne-quicklinks.com for a link to a website where you can see how people change as they grow older and read about why people age.

Friends

Friends may be quite different in some ways.

People may become friends because they have similar hobbies, interests or ideas; or just because they like each other. Friends often help each other.

Young people

Young people* are learning to manage without their parents. They often go around in groups; this gives them a feeling of belonging while being free of their families.

Old people

Old people may not be as fit as they once were but the things they have learned during their long lives can be very interesting and useful to younger people.

Countries

People living in the same country live under the same government and have to obey its laws. Laws vary from one country to another.

Alcoholic drink is banned in some countries.

Disabled people

Disabled people cannot easily do some of the things most people take for granted. There are different types of disability. Some can be overcome.

A wheelchair marathon

*To find out about children, see page 11.

21

One world

Internet link Go to **www.usborne-quicklinks.com** for a link to a website where you can play a game to find out more about saving the environment.

Humans have always had to adapt to survive and still need to adapt today. They need to change how they live before they damage the environment so much that they can no longer live in it. Here are some things they can do to improve their environment:

Clean sewage (waste from toilets and drains) properly so that it does not pollute rivers and seas.

Sewage works

Find new kinds of energy which do not pollute the air.

Wind turbines like this make electricity, without creating pollution.

Stop dumping harmful chemical waste into rivers and seas.

Make things from materials which do not harm the environment. Better still, make them from materials which can be re-used.

Bottle bank

Rare orchid

Stop letting wild animals and plants die out. As well as being important in themselves, they may be useful to humans in the future.

Use farming methods which do not damage the soil.

Stop cutting down forests. This destroys the homes of animals and plants, damages the soil and even causes changes in the weather.

Internet links

For links to more websites about people, go to the Usborne Quicklinks Website at **www.usborne-quicklinks.com** and click on the number of the website you want to visit.

Website 1 – Discover what life is like in Ghana, Russia, Brazil and India as you read photo stories about a typical day in the life of four children who live in these countries. Find out about their schooling, food, chores and dreams.

Website 2 – Read illustrated diaries written by UK children who travelled to different countries around the world to discover more about their family roots and find lots of fun facts about people, religion and food.

Website 3 – Read lots of ideas about ways you can change your shopping habits to help save the Earth's natural resources, then take a quiz and find out how Earth-friendly you and your family are.

Website 4 – The world's population is growing all the time and on this site, you can see what the population was when you were born, what it is now and what it might be in the future.

Website 5 – Find lots of fun facts about people from around the world and throughout history, and play games and quizzes.

Website 6 – Find out about different places around the world, and the people that live in them. There are descriptions of the different games people play and recipes to try out.

Index

First published in 2002 by Usborne Publishing Ltd., Usborne House, 83-85 Saffron Hill, London EC1N 8RT, England.
www.usborne.com Copyright © 2002, 1993 Usborne Publishing Ltd. The name Usborne and the device are Trade Marks of Usborne Publishing Ltd. All rights reserved. No part of this publication may be reproduced, stored in a retrieval system, or transmitted in any form or by any means, electronic, mechanical, photocopying, recording, or otherwise, without the prior permission of the publisher. Printed in China.